English Fluency For Advanced English Speaker

How to Unlock The Full Potential to Speak English Fluently

Advanced Edition

**Whitney
Nelson**

Contents

Introduction

Congratulations! You're already an advanced student of the English language. Before you take another step in your journey of learning, though, you need to pause a moment and celebrate your success thus far.

English is no easy language to learn. It's filled with idioms that make no literal sense and colloquialisms that you may only hear once in a blue moon (like the phrase I just used). If that weren't enough, there are hundreds (if not thousands) of exceptions to the established rules of grammar – especially when it comes to turning single nouns into plural nouns. The plural of alumnus is alumni, but the plural of campus is campuses. And there's really no rule you can memorize to know that except to memorize them initially. After you speak it for a while, then you get to know almost intuitively.

But you already know the challenges that face you. I'm sure you've already been swamped with many of these puzzling contradictions already. Despite all those obstacles, though, you've progressed this far, successfully encountering every twist and turn the language has thrown at you.

But, you've encountered a problem you just can't seem to solve. You've reached a plateau in your fluency. Sure, you can read the language and understand it fairly well when it's spoken quickly by native speakers. Nothing you do, however, seems to help you to make any more progress. In a phrase: you're stuck.

Stop it right there. You hear other students speak the language well. Your first thought is "Why can't I do that?"

Ahh, but you can. That's why I've written this book. It's created just for you – the advanced English student who desires to take his/her ability to speak the language to the next level.

Don't believe me?

What if I told you that armed with seven well-kept secrets you can nearly effortlessly soar to the next level of fluency in your study of English? All the struggling you've done, all the doubts you've had will fade away once your ability to speak the language you're so excited about using improves.

How can I be so sure that that these steps will work? Because not only have I used them, but thousands of others have used these same techniques to improve their skills and crack through that glass ceiling. I started sharing these secrets with interested friends, family and students. Today, they're speaking like English was their native tongue.

And you, too, can be among those successful students who discover the joy of conquering a language they once thought impossible to learn.

This Book is Not for Beginners

This book provides you with the key secrets you'll need to unlock the next level of fluency and open an entire new world of fluency. With this book by your side, you'll discover that taking your skills to the next level wasn't nearly as difficult as you originally imagined it to be.

In this book you'll not only discover the secrets, but you'll also find the encouragement to continue in your studies. As you read these pages, you'll feel as if you have your own personal English tutor sitting right next to you, guiding you every step of the way.

Having been in the same position myself at one time and helping hundreds of others in this identical situation, I have a good idea of what's running through your mind as we go through these steps.

The content of the book is arranged so that the first chapters have a general wide appeal and will help just about everyone become better at the spoken word. As you read farther in the book each section talks about the language in a bit more success. This doesn't mean that you can't understand Chapter Two without reading Chapter One. Feel free to read these chapters in any order, based on your perceived personal needs.

In the first chapter, we'll review the five myths about English that are the common obstacles of most students. You'll undoubtedly recognize at least one of them as an impediment to your learning. Once you know the myth or myths holding you back, it'll just be a matter of time to change your thinking and continue studying.

The following chapter introduces you to an effective method of creating attainable goals for yourself. Called S.M.A.R.T. goals, you'll learn how even a minimum of planning can bring a maximum of learning. You'll want to not waste a single minute implementing them in your learning schedule. Guaranteed. Not only will this goal-setting technique help you in pursuit of learning to speak the English language, but you can transfer these goal-setting skills to any dream you'd like to manifest.

The third secret to fluency is to immerse yourself in the language. Easier said than done, you say? Most students mistakenly believe that the only way to do that is to travel to meet native speakers. That's why the chapter is filled tips that'll have yourself "swimming" in English before you realize it.

None of these guidelines require travel or even walking up to total strangers and starting conversations. In fact, they all involve low-risk situations that will have you speaking English in safe, low-risk situations more often than you ever thought possible.

When you begin reading chapter four's secret to success, you may shake your head in disbelief, but by the time you've finished it you'll be eager and excited to implement suggestions. That's because this involves the one step most of us fear most when we're learning anything, not just the English language. The secret key: it's perfectly fine to make mistakes. In fact, it's not only perfectly fine, but it's nearly mandatory. It's guaranteed to change your entire way of viewing the learning process.

What does listening have to do with speaking a language? Everything! In the fifth step you'll not only discover how improving this one habit can improve your fluency by leaps and bounds. The chapter also provides you with techniques to develop your active listening skills and then translate those into the breakthrough in your speaking of English.

But that's not all, we take listening to new heights with a technique called "extensive listening." Discover how it can be the key to your breakthrough in propelling you into new English-speaking opportunities.

Then we move on to the next chapter in which you'll learn about one of the most effective methods of learning any language. Known in academic circles as shadowing, this method is also called parroting by those who use it often. Essentially, you'll be improving your fluency the way you learned your native language.

In this technique, you'll be repeating the sounds of those speaking English word for word almost at the same time the person is speaking. You'll learn how you can use this technique in a variety of situations. With today's technology, shadowing is easier than ever before.

Your Journey to Fluency

While this volume is meant to be a student's guidebook through the English language, it's really so much more. You'll find yourself referring to this book again and again in your journey of learning.

Are you prepared to climb to new levels of fluency nearly effortlessly? It's time to discover what's been keeping you on this plateau of learning. It's time to remove the obstacles in your path and seriously continue on this amazing path of learning you've set your sights on.

Let's get started!

Chapter 1: *Getting Over the Plateau to Become a Fluent English Speaker*

Are you frustrated? Do you believe you've hit the peak of your learning with regard to the English language? You can read the language. You know the grammar and you can understand it when you hear the spoken word.

Yet, you're not speaking it as fluently as you want to – as you need to. No, there's nothing wrong with you. Many persons learning English feel as you do. They've reached a certain point in their ability to speak the language and just can't seem to advance any farther.

Unfortunately, they believe that what they've learned is all that they *can* learn. They've tried and tried to reach that next level fluency but to no avail.

Does this sound like your story? Are you ready to throw up your hands and give up, thinking any more progress is hopeless? Don't quit.

But before you continue any farther, stop knocking your head against the wall. Obviously what you're doing right now is not working. It's time to step back and analyze what needs changed in your approach to learning.

Instead of going any further in your pursuit of learning the spoken English language, you need to look into your own thinking to discover if you're holding any "limiting beliefs" holding you back. These are really myths that many people hold as the truth about their ability to learn to speak English fluently that, quite frankly, just aren't true.

Here are five of the most common limiting beliefs that students of English believe are natural barriers to their learning. These "beliefs" which many attribute to holding them back from being a more fluent speaker are really nothing more but preconceived notions. They can be overcome simply by changing your thinking. Then you can break that barrier to attain the next level of fluency. It may sound a bit strange, but it really does work.

5 Myths That May Be Hindering Your English Fluency

1. Your age

This is just an excuse. At one time scientists believed that as persons aged, the harder it was for them to learn. And not just the English language, everything – math, science even the adopting of new hobbies like knitting or playing the piano.

If you think about it, that's a pretty dismal diagnosis. The standard scientific thought stated that your brain cells continued to reproduce and were receptive to learning only up to a certain age. Once you reached that age your body would no longer make any new cells. If you could learn anything new, it would be much more difficult, taking a longer period of time. Whatever it was you wanted to learn, the scientists warned you it would be an uphill battle.

The lesson people took from this dictum? If you didn't learn a language when you were younger, well you were out of luck. You weren't about to learn it as an older individual. If you did manage it, you'd be struggling every step of the way.

Today, scientists have discovered that proclamation – taken as a law for so long – is not in the least bit true.

You need to know right now that your age doesn't limit your ability to speak English fluently. It's more likely you believing your age is a limiting factor actually keeps you from learning. Once you overcome this mindset, you'll discover that English isn't as difficult to speak as you thought – and before you know it you've unlocked the secret that has prevented you from going any further.

It's time to stop blaming your age for that plateau you've reached to learn and start using the English language more. With the suggestions presented throughout the rest of this book, you'll discover that it's easier than you once believed.

2. Fear of making mistakes.

Many individuals refuse to speak English as often as they could. Why? Simply because they're afraid of making mistakes. But worse than that they believe that someone will hear them make these mistakes and laugh at them.

The thought of making a mistake when speaking English shouldn't inhibit you or limit your speaking it in any way. In fact, it really should do the exact opposite – it should spur you on to speak it all the more.

Deep down you already know what I'm about to tell you: mistakes are your friends. Making a mistake when you talk is the ultimate way to learn the English language or any language for that matter.

Every single person learning a language made some type of mistake when they started. In fact, if the truth be known, they made what they considered more than their fair share of blunders. Even native speakers don't speak perfect English. Listen closely to some native speakers and you'll see exactly what I mean.

What if I told you that instead of fearing those mistakes, you should be embracing them? Would you think I was totally insane? Well, that's exactly what you should be doing – speaking more and making more mistakes. That's because the more mistakes you make, the faster you'll learn.

Let me tell you a story about two individuals, both learning English. Both, in fact, were at about the same level of fluency. They could read and comprehend English well and in general had a good grasp of speaking it. Both wanted to go beyond where they were currently and hit the next level of fluency.

But one student feared speaking it, not only in her daily life, but also in the classroom. She would never volunteer in class and when called upon she would barely speak up. When she did answer, she used as few words as possible. The instructor continually asked her to expand on her answers.

The other student, coincidentally, was in the same classroom, and took every opportunity to speak English. He was the student always first to volunteer to answer in English. Instead of just answering with a short phrase or a one-word answer, he would make sure he'd elaborate a bit more – sometimes more than he needed to. The point is that he took every opportunity in class to speak English.

Not only that, but he would make sure he used the language as much as possible outside of the classroom as well. He made a concerted to associate with people who spoke English and made it a point to speak up in conversations even. If someone corrected his English, he thanked them. He would go on to explain that he was still learning and appreciated the corrections.

You could tell in an instant that the first student shied from talking because she feared making mistakes. She believed that every word that came out of her mouth had to be perfect. The second student, though, approached his learning not only as a positive activity, but something that was actually fun. Making mistakes didn't bother him.

You can guess who learned to speak English more quickly and more fluently. Don't let fear of making mistakes – either in class or in public – hold you back from speaking the language. We've all made mistakes – whether we're learning a language or math or any other subject. Mistakes are the foundation of any type of learning.

3. You can't remember all the rules of grammar.

Wow! Definitely don't let this hold you back. No one, not even native speakers, can remember all the grammar rules. In fact, few speakers even try to follow all the rules. This includes native English speakers. If you took the time to review all the grammar that went into speaking a sentence before you spoke it, you'd never utter another English sentence.

Instead, place your faith in your vocabulary and especially listening to others. And if you make it a point to speak English, stop holding yourself to some impossible standard; you'll never ever enjoy the language. Belief it or not, learning a new language is fun – really fun.

Perfect grammar is the last thing you need to worry about. Instead, spend your time expanding your vocabulary, learning new words and using them as much as possible in conversations. Speak English every chance you get – whether you're clear about the grammar involved in the sentences you used or not.

This book is all about speaking the English language fluently. It's not about learning grammar. It's about using the language. Let's say that you're in a group of people and want to say that you ate an apple yesterday. If your grammar is shaky you may say "I yesterday apple eat."

Don't worry about making a fool of yourself. A native speaker may correct you and tell you the sentence is structured like this: "I ate an apple yesterday." Poof! You've learned to speak the language a little better through speaking up. And now you actually have a pattern for speaking a sentence like that.

You've learned first how to pattern a sentence in the past tense. You've also learned that the past tense of eat is "ate."

In that small insignificant mistake, you've broken through to the next level.

And the best part is that you didn't have to struggle over any grammar rules. All in all, you probably now feel better about yourself. Not only for speaking up but for actually learning how to use English grammar at the same time. Imagine how quickly you can improve your grammar without even thinking about it just by speaking a few sentences. Imagine what would happen if you spoke even more.

Instead of holing yourself up in your house and studying the dizzying array of grammar rules before you speak, get together with English speakers – native speakers and students like yourself – and use the vocabulary you've already learned.

4. You need to travel to be able to speak English fluently.

Another fallacy. You don't need to travel anywhere in order to improve your speech. There are many people who have learned the English language without going very far from home. If you're already living in the United States, that's not so much an issue, anyway.

But if you're currently living outside an English-speaking country and learning the language with an eye to visiting such a country in the near future you may view learning English is a hopeless pursuit. You may also be re-assessing why you're even bothering to learn the language.

Don't start second-guessing yourself. You can learn the language from wherever you are at the moment even if you don't have access to what you think you need. Have access to a computer? Then you already know how many video clips are on the web in English. Listen to these, repeat what these speakers say and the way they say it. Imagine these speakers are in the same room with you.

If you have to, stop the video and repeat what they've said, then double check yourself. There are plenty of ways of learning English – and as long as you're learning, there is no wrong way.

The key here is to focus on learning it using a method that's available for you. Instead of mourning that you can't travel or you don't know anyone who is speaking the language, dig around on the internet and find an English-speaking site. You may even discover a site that teaches you English. There are certainly plenty out there.

5. There are no other people around me speaking English.

This is a corollary to the "I can't travel to an English speaking country" myth. While it certainly would be easier if you knew individuals who could speak English, it's definitely not essential – regardless of what you've heard to the contrary.

With a computer keyboard at your fingertips, and the internet, it doesn't matter whether you live with or next door to English speakers or not. With less effort than you'd ever imagine on your part, you can find someone who speaks English.

Not only that, I'm betting that you'll also discover students of English – just like yourself – who are looking for others who speak at their level of fluency. Imagine how much you all could help each other. Imagine how much you can learn with only a bit of effort on your part.

These are the five most common complaints that people use to block their excelling at speaking the English language like a native. How many of these apply to you?

What Are Your Personal Myths?

Do you have any other personally limiting beliefs that hold you back from learning to speak the English language? If you do, why not stop right now and write them down. Now study them really well. Are those really valid reasons for not learning the English language? Can you think of any way you can overcome them?

Regardless of what your personal thoughts are about your inability to get to the next level of English fluency, remember that the only thing that is holding you back are your beliefs. The moment you believe you can learn to speak the English language like a native, you will.

It's time to think more positively about your ability to improve your ability to speak the English language. Just changing your thinking from "Wow! This is really difficult," to "Hey, this is getting easier all the time!" will help you speak more fluently. Guaranteed.

Chapter 2: Setting S.M.A.R.T. Goals -- The Secret of Getting What You Want When You Want It

Pedro complained to his English instructor one day that he was disappointed that his fluency in the language seemed to have hit a peak. "I can't advance any farther," he said, "and I'm far from sounding like a native speaker. And that is the long run is my goal. Did I set my sights too high?"

The instructor told him that, indeed, he did not set any goal that he could not accomplish; he just may have to re-think how to reach them. That's when he told Pedro about S.M.A.R.T. goals.

Are you feeling "stuck" in your level of learning? Are you, like Pedro, beginning to think you'll never break through to that next level of learning in which you sound more fluent – more like a native speaker?

Then perhaps it's time you look into using S.M.A.R.T. goals as well. What are they? What make SMART goals different from any other? Simple. When you create this type of goal, you're strategically placing yourself in a position of achieving them. If you follow the guidelines of these techniques, in fact, it would be extremely difficult to fail.

S.M.A.R.T

I can hear you now, "When do we start?" Well, there's no time like the present. S.M.A.R.T. is an acronym for Specific, Measurable, Attainable, Responsible and Time-Bound. If you make your goals in accordance with these five guidelines, you're well on your way to fulfilling your English-language dreams.

But more than that, this is a technique used by a growing number of business executives as well as entrepreneurs to move their projects forward. It's time tested. And the best part is that you can take these guidelines and use them for any goals you have for your life.

The letter "S" in S.M.A.R.T. stands for specific. You've probably created many goals in your life. Think back to several of them. Think about the times you succeeded as well as those instances in which you didn't reach them. What made the difference? What did you do right when you achieved your goals? How did this differ from the times you didn't reach your dreams?

Perhaps it could be that the ones you achieved were worded more specifically. Did you know exactly what you wanted? This works regardless of what your goals are—they aren't necessarily related to your learning the English language.

Take, for example, the individual who wanted to lose weight. She started out by saying that "someday" she'd like to lose weight. But until she decided specifically how many pounds she wanted to lose, her weight held steady. Once she made the decision and gave herself a deadline, however, she couldn't understand why she couldn't stick to an eating plan.

So your first step is deciding specifically what it is you want to do. Once you know exactly what it is, then create specific steps you believe will get you there. Let's say your goal is to be able to speak English well enough to make a presentation in front of your supervisors and several department managers at work..

Now write down what you believe you need to do in order to speak English well enough to do it. These are your steps for reaching your goals. For example, if giving a presentation is the goal, you must look critically at your spoken language skills now.

Decide what type of improvements you need to make. You may decide you

- Want to work on your pronunciation
- Learn more vocabulary words – as well as perfect their pronunciation
- Learn how to tell a joke in English

What else do you believe is keeping you from reaching this level of fluency in the English language. Not sure? Ask your instructor or a trusted friend.

Make sure you keep a list of these, because you'll going to need them for the next step. Keeping in mind your goal of making this presentation, we'll go to the next step in S.M.A.R.T. goals

The M in S.M.A.R.T. goals stands for measurable. That may be a no-brainer when it's said that way, but you'd be surprised how many people create goals without thinking about how they're going to measure their progress. And if you can't measure whether you're a quarter of the way to your goal or half to making your dream come true, how will you ever know when you've reached that particular goal?

That's why you need to discover a way to measure your progress. Let's continue with the example we used in the previous paragraphs. You want to perfect your ability to speak English so you can give a presentation at work.

The first thing we listed that needed to be improved was your ability to pronounce English.

Let's say this is your goal as well. Just saying it doesn't get it done. You could spend years perfecting it, but never recognize when your speech is, indeed, good enough. Your first decision – and creating a measurable goal – is to either recognize your improvement yourself or getting someone's opinion on your pronunciation. Ideally, this would be your instructor. If you don't have an ,rn to your English mentor or a trusted friend.

You see how by adding this idea of measuring your improvement, you've created a goal you can work toward – and feel good about attaining once you've reached it.

Your second step in speaking English well enough to make a presentation was expand your vocabulary. Here again you need to set a certain number of words you want to learn and to pronounce. If you don't settle on how many words, you could be learning words forever. So not only settle on how many, but perhaps pick out a few from an English book, or ask your English teacher for recommendations on a few words. You may even want to ask a few colleagues what type of words they would recommend that may be business related.

Within this, you'll then want to start tackling this list. In addition to having friends and tutors help with your pronunciation, remember the web – especially any dictionary applications or sites you have access to. The definition each entry provides you with a proper pronunciation of the word.

And finally one of your goals was to be able to tell a joke. How are you going to turn this into a measurable goal? You may want to practice in front of the mirror or with a good friend who'll be honest with you. Once you've earned the thumbs of a friend you may want to take your joke to several more people to get their opinions.

The key to success in creating any successfully measurable goal is to look at the details of what needs to be done and honestly evaluate your ability to do it. Making the decision on how to measure your progress is a big step in ensuring this will work.

While you should never give up your dream, you also need to be open to the process of making it measurable as well as creating the best possible strategy to make this happen You also need to continually reassess how vital these goals are to you.

Now that you have one or more goals that are specific measurable, your next step is to ensure that your goals are attainable   Yes, the A in S.M.A.R.T. goals stand for attainable.

This is an important aspect of creating any goal – not just those related to your speaking English. This step may take some time. First, you need to be absolutely honest with yourself. What do you truly believe you can attain. Don't overstretch your reach and set some impossible goal that is beyond your level. That will only disappoint you and you may wrongly believe learning English is simply beyond your capability.

It's better to set a goal and break it into two steps and reach it than set one that's simply impossible to reach. Let's face it I'm five foot two inches tall. If my goal were to play professional basketball that may be seen as an unattainable goal. But to set a goal that I make so certain percentage of the shots I take on the court is attainable for me. That goal involves more my skill more than my natural height.

Pedro, for example, originally set a goal of learning how to pronounce fifteen new words a week. Before he committed himself to that goal, though, he thought long and hard if it really were attainable. Having second thoughts, he instead set his sights on learning ten – at least for the first week. After that, he would adjust his goal depending on how he performed the first week.

When you're working with the idea of whether your goals are attainable, you may have to be flexible. If you discover that you set your sights a bit too high, reduce them. There's no shame in doing that. In fact, having a desire that is at least realistic will help build your self-confidence.

On the other hand, you don't want to make your target so easy that it doesn't challenge you. If your goal is too easy, you won't push yourself to do your best – and you may even lose interest.

Pedro may also want to create an attainable goal that he can meet with a teacher or close friend weekly to help him with his speaking. Once a week, for example, sounds reasonable. If he set his sights on meeting with someone five times a week that may be a bit excessive and end up being something he couldn't achieve – which would possibly make him feel as if he failed. In reality, he really didn't fail, he simply underestimated the time involved in meetings like that.

Pedro gave much thought to how to perfect telling a joke and the attainability of that goal as well. He admired several comedians on television. The question he had to ask himself was should he hold himself up to a professional level of delivery when he wasn't even a native speaker.

The fact of the matter was that he admired the presentations of several of his colleagues who had told some great jokes. The attainable goal, then, would be to practice until he felt he could present more like them. He thought that would be an attainable goal.

He could learn to pitch these jokes through various ways – including professionals on television as well as the colleagues you work with. Pedro also recorded himself telling the joke to review his pronunciation.

Not only does Pedro have to learn to be flexible, he has to discover what smaller, equally attainable, goals he break this dream into smaller chunks.

The letter R in S.M.A.R.T. goals stands for the word responsible. The question becomes who is responsible for achieving this goal. The obvious answer is Pedro. As you create your goals, it will become quite apparent that you are ultimately responsible. What Pedro learned as he went along, however, was he needed to hold those who offered services of their help responsible as well.

He would have difficulty attaining some of the goals without the help of his friends, colleagues and instructors. This by no means absolves him of all responsibility for achieving them, but it does mean he may have to ensure in some from that those who offered to help him actually do.

If that should occur, he may have to take the imitative in reminding his instructor or others that they had volunteered to help. He may have to suggest times they could meet. Pedro can't – and neither can you – just ask for help and then expect them to always take the initiative to help you.

Other issues that may fall under the responsible portion of the S.M.A.R.T. goals include the amount of time you can realistically invest in each goal. Hold yourself responsible for ensuring you've created goals that over extend you or your resources. If you set unrealistic goals, you'll be disappointed and tempted to give up.

You'll also have to approach your goals responsibly. A large part of that is knowing when to ask for help. It could be that you need someone to spend time with you and assess your pronunciation. It could also be something as simple as an individual who you report to occasionally who holds you accountable for your progress.

The T of the acronym of S.M.A.R.T. represents the phrase time-bound. Have you ever heard the saying that goals without a deadline are dreams? While it's admirable to have dreams, the word itself implies that it's something that you'll see fulfilled in the future. Or worse yet something that's totally unachievable.

You're not dealing with pie-in-the-sky dreams that you don't expect to come true. Not by a long shot. You're creating specific targets that you expect to reach. When can you expect to see these goals manifest? That's up to you.

One thing is one hundred percent certain, though: if you don't hold yourself to a deadline, they'll never materialize. Pedro discovered this. He found that if he didn't put a specific time to reach his goal, he was far less likely to actually achieve them.

Pedro, for example, knew that it would take some time before he would be able to master the English language well enough to present a project report to his colleagues at work. So he set his sights on achieving them in one year.

But he also knew that he had to do the same thing with the intermediate goals that would eventually get him to his dream. So he sat down with pencil and a calendar in order to start assigning a timeline to his smaller goals.

In order to do this correctly, he needed to analyze the smaller goals and set an attainable time line for all of his goals. The moment he realized that he would be running behind on one of the smaller aims, he then would need to re-evaluate all the goals which followed. It could mean that he would encounter a chain reaction. All the steps after that one would also be met later than he had intended.

If he encountered this, he could handle this is two ways. First, he could just delay the attainment of these steps and assignment himself a later manifestation day. Or, he could adjust his goals – even if it means working a bit harder and longer – in order to reach his ultimate goal on time.

The point of setting specific completion dates is that it helps you to plan. Pedro set a final target date as one year. A year from the day he started he hoped to be standing in front of his colleagues informing them about the progress of a project. If he saw he was falling behind on this timetable, he could then adjust his intermediate steps to recover some of the lost time.

Being held time-bound for a goal is also a great motivating factor to aid in your planning. Once Pedro set a final goal, he worked backwards in planning deadlines for all the smaller steps. He started with his final goal date and carefully charted where he had a be a month before his final goal and then two months before that date.

He actually spent quite a bit of time figuring out how much time he'd need for all the smaller steps needed in order to get where he wanted to be on time.

Pedro decided that in a week he should work on one lesson on vocabulary – learning the meaning of the words. Additionally, he needed to put in two practice sessions on pronunciation. One of those would be conducted on his own with the help of a recorder and the internet and one would be – when possible – with his instructor or a good friend.

The final decision Pedro made in fulfilling the time bound portion of the S.M.A.R.T. goals was to take a few moments periodically in order to assess his progress. He set his assessment dates as once a month. He compared where he was to where he hoped to be. Was he on track? Would he be able to make his goal within the time frame he set? Or was he running behind?

Did he need to increase the number of vocabulary words he was learning every week or did he need more work on his pronunciation. Whatever he eventually decided, he fine-tuned his schedule to accommodate his ultimate completion date.

S.M.A.R.T goals are an excellent method of ensuring you don't lose sight of your desires. How many times have set New Year's resolutions only to find by February, you realize you're not working toward them? That's because you didn't apply the follow up work necessary to keep you laser focused on your goal. You merely wrote down some vague goal and went on with your life. Your New Year's resolutions become nothing more than afterthoughts as you continued on with your life.

You can easily see how setting – and maintaining – S.M.A.R.T. goals are essential in manifesting your desire to speak English fluently. The key to working these goals is to keep them uppermost in your mind. Pedro learned – and so you'll discover this as well – that learning English is a daily discipline. You can't learn to speak fluently by cramming a week's worth of work into a day or two.

The Need for Flexibility

The other lesson Pedro learned from instituting this technique is that he needed to maintain a degree of flexibility. If a step isn't working, then he needed to revise it. If he hadn't progress as far as he had hoped by the end of a month or so, he needed to re-assess his strategy. He needed to analyze what was working and what wasn't. and he needed to do it on a regular basis.

But there is one more action Pedro took when he successfully completed each of his smaller goals. He rewarded himself. At the very least, he stopped for a few moments and told himself how good he was doing. Sometimes, he would treat himself to a dinner out or buy himself a small present.

You should consider doing something similar. It needn't be a large purchase or even a huge dinner. The important thing is that you stop for several moments and compliment yourself on doing a good job. Then cheer yourself on to going all the way.

Once you've set your goals, it's time to move on to learning methods on achieving these goals. In the next chapter you'll learn that the fastest way to learn English is to just dive into the language. You'll also learn some techniques on doing just that.

Chapter 3: Immerse Yourself in the English Language

Have you ever wondered what the difference is between an individual who seems to glide through learning the English language and someone who struggles with every word – perhaps even every syllable?

You may have assumed that's it a matter of skill. You dismiss their success as a natural talent they possess for learning the spoken word. You may even credit them with being smarter than the average person.

Well, you may think all of that, but you'd be wrong. Those who learn how to speak English fluently are neither smarter than you nor do they necessarily have a gift for learning languages.

What separates those who learn the spoken word of English from those who don't can be described in one word: immersion.

What? Those who seem to learn effortlessly simply immerse themselves into the language. They seek out opportunities to speak English at every turn. If they have to make a choice between speaking their native language or English, they choose English every chance they get.

Consider this for a moment. You'll never improve at any activity – jogging, playing piano or even knitting – unless you practice. Practicing the English language is the only way to immerse yourself in the language.

The Only Way to Learn English

Believe it or not, you can be the person who others envy at your quick grasp of the English language. You can be the individual who speaks it with ease. And you can start right now. As long as you keep these guidelines in mind.

1. Don't spend a lot of time perfecting your grammar.

Believe it or not, this is probably *the most important rule in learning how to speak English.*

Your goal isn't to write a paragraph in English with no grammatical mistakes. You goal is to speak it. So don't obsess with grammar. If you listen closely to native speakers not everyone speaks English perfect all the time.

Let's face it, at this point in your studies you already have a firm grasp of English grammar. You probably could even correct a native speaker when they don't use proper grammar. So, if your goal is to become a better speaker you need to focus on using it as if it were your first language.

Actually, studying grammar will only hinder your development using the spoken word. If you analyze what you're about to say and think about all the grammar rules before you speak, you'll discover the precise moment to say what you wanted to.

When you're thinking about this guideline you need to know that even most native speakers of the English language only know about 20 percent of all the hundreds (and hundreds) of the rules. A mere 20 percent. At this point in your studies, you probably already know more than that.

Don't worry, the more frequently you speak English, you'll undoubtedly get an ear for proper grammar. After a while, the sound of an improperly structured sentence or verbs that don't agree with you subject will sound horrible. As long as you know what sounds right, you'll be able to speak it well enough. I'm guessing that, as an advanced student, you already have a grasp of this aspect of your learning.

2. Learn phrases, not words.

Think about it. You probably know many vocabulary words. And you undoubtedly know how to pronounce them. But what you really need to study at this point are phrases. While knowing the words are, indeed, important, languages are really a compilation of phrases.

I'm sure you know students of the language who have an impeccable grasp of vocabulary words but still can't create a sentence if their life depended on it. Why? They failed to study English phrases.

When children learn how to talk, they're definitely immersed in their native language. It's usually the only language they hear from the moment they wake up until they're tucked into bed at night. What they hear are not separate words, but sentences, phrases and everything in between.

If you already know about 1,000 words (and you probably know more than that right now), you could still find yourself stumbling over stringing more than two sentences together to engage yourself intelligently in conversation.

But all you really need to know is approximately 100 phrases and you'll be able to string sentence after sentence with ease. In contrast you'll be surprised how much more fluent you'll be. If you know 1,000 separate words, you may be able to correctly create one sentence. Only one sentence.

If you learn 100 phrases you'll be able to speak many more sentences. And if you get ambitious and learn 1,000 phrases (it's not nearly as difficult as it seems) . . . well . . . you'll be nearly as fluent as a native speaker.

Once you learn even a few of these phrases a week, your understanding of speaking this language with explode exponentially. The trick is to learn the phrase so well that you only have to exert a small amount effort on completing them.

Listed below are several of the most common phrases in the language. How many of them do you know? If you find there are some you're stumbling over, then you may want to study those some.

- *How often do you (plus verb)?*
- *Can I help you (plus verb or as a question by itself)?*
- *It's too late for that*
- *You could have (plus a verb)*

- *If I were you I would have (add verb)*
- *It looks like (plus a noun)*
- *It's time to (plus a verb)*
- *What if (plus a subject and verb)*
- *How was (plus a noun)*
- *Let's say that (plus subject and verb)*
- *I think I should (plus a verb)*
- *I'm sorry to (plus a verb)*
- *I was thinking about (plus a verb)*
- *I think I should (plus a verb)*
- *Thank you for (plus a verb)*
- *I don't know what to do about (plus a noun)*
- *Have you ever thought about (plus a verb)?*

Using just one of those phrases, you're about to see how many different situations it's suited for:

Have you ever thought about (plus a verb)?

- Have you ever thought about starting your business?
- Have you ever thought about changing jobs?
- Have you ever thought about learning how to swim?
- Have you ever thought about becoming a writer?
- Have you ever thought about having more children?
- Have you ever thought about selling your house?
- Have you ever thought about visiting South America?
- Have you ever thought about learning Russian?
- Have you ever thought about the meaning of life?
- Have you ever thought about joining a fitness center?

If you learned just this one phrase, you can immediately see how many ways you can use it in daily conversation. This phrase, in particular, is a great example, because when you ask it, you're inviting someone into a conversation with you.

That will spawn the use of even more sentences using phrases you've already learned.

Can you see how pointless it becomes to learn individual words when your ultimate aim is to speak more fluently? That's not to say that learning more words isn't important. But don't forget to give a priority to learning phrases as well.

3. Think in English

When you go to speak to someone, don't think in your native language and then translate your sentence into English. Simply think in English. This is one of those guidelines that is easier said than done. You're trying to break a habit – thinking in your native tongue – that has been with you all of your life. To be honest, you probably don't know any other way to think.

Why is thinking in your native language not a particularly good idea? The ordering of the words in your native language is more than language not going to be the same as in the English language. Your natural tendency will be to repeat the English words in that order.

But more than that, in the process of translating your sentence, you'll probably be trying to use grammar rules you're not all that familiar with yet.

Thinking in English will, undoubtedly be difficult at first, but the more you force your mind to do it, easier it becomes. And the easier it becomes, the more fluent you'll be at the English language. Give it a try the next time you go to speak English.

4. Practice speaking English when you hear it.

Remember that reading and listening to the English word doesn't make you a better speaker. It will give you more knowledge of reading the written word and understanding it when it is spoken to you. But learning to speak it yourself, requires you do more work. It requires that you truly become interactive with the language.

Without a doubt, reading and listening to the language are two of the most important aspects of learning English. But you're missing the final piece of the puzzle if you don't practice speaking it. This goes for any language, not just English.

Think about the order in which young children learn their native language. They first learn how to speak it and become quite fluent in it and finally learn how to read. Yes, I know that in the process they make many grammatical mistakes. One of the most common is to use the word "brung" as a past tense form of "bring." The correct form is brought. "Look what I've brung you." But the vital point is they didn't wait until they knew what the proper form of the verb was before they spoke. And they do indeed get their message across.

So, don't obsess with reading and listening. It appears the natural order of learning a language is listening, speaking, reading and then writing. So don't think for a moment that your reading and writing skills aren't good enough to allow you to speak it. Your average four-year-old doesn't seem to worry about it.

5. Surround yourself with others who speak English

I've said it before and I'll say it again: immerse yourself in the English language. Compare the English language to an ocean. As long as you stay on the ship you'll only learn what's at the surface of the ocean. Sure, you'll have a great view of the waves and you know the temperature by dipping your hands in the water occasionally. But you'll never know what lies beneath the surface unless you immerse yourself – submerge yourself – into the body of water.

If you don't the plunge from the boat into the ocean right now, when will you?
Think about this for a moment. Those English students who excel at speaking the language are usually the individuals who attended – or are still attending – an English-speaking school. Why is that? Because they were in a culture that forced them to speak English. If they had their way they might have preferred to speak more in their own language.

But they took all their classroom lessons in English, talked to their professors in English – even talked to their friends in English.

Compare these individuals to those who studied abroad, but returned lamenting they still aren't fluent in the language. Because all the while they were in an English-speaking country they never allowed themselves to take the plunge. For whatever reason, they never took the plunge into fully using what skills they had developed up to that time?

So does that mean you have to travel or go to an English-speaking school in order to speak the language fluently? No, not by a long shot. You can become fluent in the language without ever traveling anywhere! Simply make a pact with your friends who are also learning the language that you're all going to dive into the ocean of English to learn what's beneath the surface.

Promise each other then when gathered you'll only speak English. Don't have that many friends who are English speakers or learning the language? Before you know it you'll find yourself thinking in English when you're around these individuals and speaking in the language won't seem so frightening any longer.

Chapter 4: Mistakes Are the Foundation Of Any Good Speaker

"Would you like me to give you a formula for success? It's quite simple, really.
Double your rate of failure."
—Thomas J. Watson, founder of IBM

Right about now, you may be thinking that this chapter is a thinly veiled attempt to make you believe that mistakes are good. They're our "friends" in fact. You may also be thinking that I'm crazy.

But it's true. Mistakes are your "friends." I hate to tell you but the sooner you recognize this, the faster you'll learn the English language.

If you've ever heard any motivational speaker, then you've probably heard that you can only learn if you're willing to make mistakes. This statement is true regardless of what you're doing learning a language to building a multimillion dollar business.

The speaker, of course, didn't mean that you should purposely set out to make mistakes. What he meant was when you find you've made a mistake, learn from it and continue on.

It's the greatest advice you can be given, in fact, with regard to learning how to speak English. You can only be a fluent speaker if you actual speak it. When you do speak it you're very likely to make mistakes, it's only natural.

In a way, you could say if you're not making any mistakes then you're really not learning much. You may think that's a harsh statement, but it happens to be the truth.

When you hit that plateau of speaking English, then it's vital to break through to the next level as quickly as possible. And the only way to do that is to expose yourself to the possibility of making mistakes in your speech.

For most of us that means to step outside of your comfort zone. That's a scary proposition for most of us. But you know you have to do it. The following are a few tips of how to practice speaking more despite your fears.

1. Enter a low-risk situation

What's a low-risk situation? It's one that's friendly enough that when you do make mistakes, those around understand and gently correct you. It's a situation in which you trust those with whom you're speaking to understand you're learning.

One of the best situations to put yourself into is to work with other students. You need to ask everyone in the conversation to correct you – diplomatically, of course – when you misspeak or your grammar is horribly incorrect. You, in turn, are confronting your fear and leaving your comfort zone in a limited, controlled way.

So what produces this fear anyway? It seems counter-intuitive that you would fear speaking the very language you've been so enthusiastic about learning. But that's human nature.

You're not alone in your fear. And if you understand the origin of your fear, then you'll be able to grapple with it better. Many psychologists will tell you that the fear of doing something, even learning a language, stems from your thinking that you must speak it perfectly. That is without any mistakes.

You need to ask yourself why you feel this way. What would happen if you did make a mistake in your conversation? The worst-case scenario would be being laughed at, let's say. Your mistake may unintentionally offend someone. Or it may mean that someone misunderstood what your said.

There may be other reasons though you fear mistakes when speaking to others. Perhaps you have the long-held belief that making a mistake is a sign of weakness.

The problem with this line of thinking, though, is that you have molded these thoughts to such gigantic proportions and distorted them so they're all you can see. Now, you've created the mindset that you can't afford the "luxury" of making a mistake in your conversations.

Does this scenario apply to you? If the perfectionist line of thinking is hindering your learning you *can* change your thinking with three easy steps and start speaking English again.

1. First you need to identify this type of thinking.

This means you must give some thought to why you're hesitating about speaking English in public. Have you been laughed at in the past for mistakes you've made? Perhaps, in making a mistake you've inadvertently offended someone. Now, you're afraid of offending any more individuals.

If you can identify why you're fearful of speaking in public, then you can start to design a strategy to conquer it.

2. List other ways of thinking about this

Once you know the catalyst of your fears, then create a list of other ways of thinking about your speaking English with others. This could include such thoughts as, "Others understand that I'm still learning and will forgive my mistakes," "The more I speak the better I'll become and the fewer mistakes I'll make," "I need to accept these mistakes myself and not only forgive myself for them, but learn from them as well."

3. Now review this list of alternative thoughts. Compare it to your perfectionist thinking.

Once you analyze both ways of thinking see if you can't develop another perspective on the situation that will be helpful to your learning and give you a more realistic view of the situation.

It may take some time to change your thinking, but you can if you follow these suggestions. You may even begin speaking a limited amount while you're reviewing your situation.

I have a friend who's still learning English. He speaks it fairly well, but the one situation he hates to find himself in is ordering pizza over the phone. He's terrified he'll order the wrong toppings and he then has a worthless pizza.

So this is how he used these steps to reduce his fears about it. After he calmed down a bit from the thought, he identified his perfectionist thinking: "The person taking my order will think I'm stupid."

He then created alternative thoughts to counter that: "I'm anything but stupid." "I'm using a new language that's not my native tongue." "I'm speaking English the best I can at this point." "Speaking on the phone is a wonderful way to use my English skills." "In fact, the more I take risks like this, the more natural my speaking skills will be," "The more I speak the language, the better I'll be and the more confident I'll be."

Then he evaluated the situation in a new light: "I may be afraid of looking stupid. But I know differently. I'm learning a new language and I'm giving it my best shot. I'm allowed to make mistakes. It is, after all, the only way I'll improve."

And improve you will. The more often you step out of your comfort zone and push yourself to speak English, you'll discover that your English is getting better and better. Why not try it yourself? What have you got to lose – except your fear, that is?

Are You Ready to Accelerate the Learning Process?

Yes, I am talking about mistakes. Just like the individual above you finally took the risk of ordering pizza in English, it's time you take that giant leap to not only accepting your mistakes, but embracing them. You've probably heard the story about Thomas Edison, probably the most prolific inventor of the twentieth century. He was asked once how he felt during his failed attempts at finding the proper material for the filament of the light bulb. The individual specifically pointed out that Edison went through nearly 10,000 various materials before he discovered the proper one.

Edison quickly corrected him with this unique perspective on the situation: "I did not fail 9,999 times. I found 9,999 ways of how not to create a light bulb."

As long as you view your mistakes as signs for not learning or reasons why you'll never learn to speak the language, you'll never go beyond the level of fluency you're at right now.

The moment, however, you accept mistakes as not only a natural part of life, but a very necessary tool in the learning process, you'll unleash that hidden power of learning that lies within you.

Now is the time to accept the power of mistakes and press on and expose yourself as often as possible to the English language. Do this not fearful of making mistakes, but vowing to embrace the mistakes and learning from them. This, more than any other piece of advice, will radically change your view of learning the English language.

Here are a few tips to start you off:

1. Find a trusted partner to work with

You can spend all the time you want reading English, but the moment you do you've expanded your world of learning. Grab a partner that's ideally at your level of fluency or better. The idea is to create an atmosphere for learning that embraces – even encourages – mistakes. If you're both at about the same level of development, then you'll discover that you'll be benefit from this partnership.

When you're searching for your partner, don't fear from asking someone you know from the internet or a friend in another part of the country. You can always practice the language through the technology of Skype.

You may also want to spend some time exploring the web site sharedtalk.org. Here, you'll discover not only students of the English language, but native speakers as well. In addition to chat rooms, the site contains "voice rooms," where several individuals can go to comfortably practice the language.

There's just one word of caution in this method. That's the fact that you must find a person who embraces the possibility of mistakes as you do. You both need to know you have that freedom.

2. Refine and expand your learning

Once you've found your partner then it's time to get down to business. You may believe that sitting and talking is an excellent exercise. But think a moment about taking the extra step. Expand and refine your learning by through several strategies.

One of them is to purposely ask your partner to pronounce a few of the vocabulary words you've been using. Then repeat the words after him or her. This works extremely well if your language partner is a native speaker. He'll know the nuances of the spoken word that someone who speaks English as a second language may not.

Another trick to getting the most out of these sessions is to record them, with the permission of your language buddy of course. Then you make reviewing this recording a priority of your next study session when you're alone.

This will take certainly enhance your learning capacity. Even though you believe you'll never forget both the mistakes you made as well as the proper way to speak the words, don't count on it. Your ability to retain all of this information in this situation is limited – and no, not because you're not bright enough.

Rather, in this type of situation your mind is reassessing and processing so many different things, that not everything you learned in this session may get transferred along to that not everything you learned in this session may get transferred along to our long-term memory. Once you play this information back on a recorder, you'll undoubtedly encounter something you had completely forgotten about.

3. Talk about interesting subjects

What's worse than being engaged in a boring conversation? Being engaged in a boring conversation in which you're still learning the language.

I guarantee you that if you don't choose topics that fully engage you, two things will occur. First, you'll become incredibly bored with the conversation. Second, you'll cut the session short as soon as you get the chance.

But by choosing a topic that you're already interested in – ideally passionate about – you'll discover that you can talk on forever. Not only that but you'll be far less fearful about making mistakes. You'll also be eager to expand your vocabulary and pronunciation of new words.

Fluency in any language is only possible if you learn the subtle art of listening. Don't expect to gain much knowledge if when you do get a chance to speak in English you're too nervous to listen or to busy translating what the others are saying to concentrate on the meaning of the words and the course of the conversation. We discuss this in more depth in the following chapter.

Chapter 5: Improve Your Listening, Your Fluency Will Follow

It's nearly impossible to talk about enhancing your fluency in English without talking about the act of listening. The two are intertwined. The only way to truly speak the language like a native is to listen to those who already speak it well.

While you may believe you've been "listening" all this time, perhaps it's time to dig into what's involved in the listening process – especially the more advanced listening skills that every language student needs. It's actually not extremely difficult to develop these skills. If you simply keep your mind on the conversation at hand, then you're already far along in improving your active listening skills.

There are many reasons to develop such skills, even beyond that of learning a language. Listening is actually a fundamental method of learning knowledge of any type. Think about it, when you were in school you needed to learn how to listen to your instructor or your professor. If you didn't actively listen, you may have found yourself struggling in class.

Active listening in a classroom setting means not only understanding what your teacher is saying, but even taking notes on the topic, in order to take a test at a later date.

Once you progress into the business world, you'll discover the ability to listen actively will help you understand customers, clients and colleagues alike.

It should come as no surprise then that active listening is an important aspect in learning how to speak the language. It's how you'll learn what syllables to emphasize in certain words, how to structure sentences and how to make plural nouns out of single nouns. And that's just for starters.

As you go along, you'll soon be recognizing idioms and colloquialisms. And before you know it, you'll be not only understanding them, but using them yourself.

Tips for Enhancing your Active Listening Skills

1. Face the speaker, make eye contact and watch him speak

This is excellent advice for anyone engaged in a conversation. It's especially important for those involved in business. In fact, you may already have developed this habit if you've conducted any type of business in your native language. But this advice is critical to an individual learning the language.

What do you gain by listening this way? Watching him speak will help you see how he forms words with his mouth so you can do the same when you use those words.

2. Pay attention to what the person is saying, but stay relaxed.

Perhaps this is the hardest advice of all when it comes to attentive listening and learning the English language. After all, you're going to be nervous, just making sure you understand what he's saying. It's difficult to stay relaxed, but if you can do just that, you'll actually increase your power of learning.

3. Mentally screen out all distractions

Background noises and movements of those around you are considered distractions. Once you begin to focus on what the English-speaking individual is saying, you'll probably find this comes naturally to you.

If you do find your mind wandering, simply bring it back to the present moment and the speaker. Don't waste any time or energy belittling yourself for your slip up.

4. Listen to the words being said and visualize what the speaker is saying

This is an effective way of immersing yourself in the language. It allows your mind to create relate words and images and will help you with your ability to actually think in English. Not only that, but you'll also discover that when you do that, you'll retain the information longer.

After all, what good is learning the language if you don't retain what you're learning?

5. Summarize what the other person has said

In many ways, this is the ultimate test of how well you understand the spoken word. But more than that, by paraphrasing and summarizing what you believe you've just heard, you're actually using all your skills in speaking. Speaking on your feet challenges you to think in English, something you need to learn in order to speak the language better.

Beyond Active Listening

But if that's as far as you've taken your listening skills, then you're actually cheating yourself. You're holding yourself back from quicker, easier fluency in the English language. That's because there's a skill beyond active listening and it's called extensive listening. If you've never heard it, then it's time you not only learn what it is, but how to use it to your advantage.

Extensive listening is an amazing tool you can use in practicing your skills at listening to others speak the English language. Basically it involves taking a topic and listening to it presented in a myriad of different forms – recordings, videos and interviews, both live and recorded.

If you had to make one change or add one thing to your learning program, including extensive listening would be the item. It's easy enough to start.

Choose a topic that interests you. If you read the last chapter and have a favorite subject matter you're already talking with your language partner with, it could be that. The alternative is to select a different topic. Consider though how you can expand your language skills if you used the same topic for each exercise.

Whatever topic it is, two things will help you excel at this challenge. The first is to make sure that it's a subject you'll be able to find a good deal of material on. Second, try to make it a topic you're already have at least a passing knowledge on. This will definitely facilitate your learning.

Once you've chosen your topic, then begin to research it. You'll be searching for resources that require you to listen. That means reading articles at this point, at least, is not a priority. Think YouTube videos, podcasts, television documentaries and even radio talk shows.

When you listen, especially at first, listen to comprehend the main ideas. At this point, don't worry about many of the details. If you can understand and repeat the important points of the topic, you're doing great.

Choose sources, by the way, that emphasize the basic information. If you delve too far into the topic, you may discover that you become frustrated, especially if it involves the learning of a specialized vocabulary. Of course, the more advanced you are when you start this exercise the more you can dig into the topic.

You may find yourself discarding one topic and choosing another. The initial subject may be beyond your language skills at the moment, or you may find the subject matter to easy depending where you are in your learning.

Keep in mind during this challenge, that extensive listening is probably the most difficult thing for a language student to do so be prepared to dedicate yourself to this technique.

Not sure what topic to select for this exercise? Below are several general selections. You can begin exploring these to see if anything interests you. In the process, though, it's very likely you'll discover even more interesting topics you'd like to pursue:

1. News stories and biographical information on political leaders and international sports stars.

2. Reviews given in English of movies or television programs you've watched in your language.

Thanks to the internet and the myriad of cable networks that the average person is exposed to today, this is an easy topic to research. From here, you may discover an interest in one of the actors or actresses and expand your horizons.

If you're not quite sure where to look for listening material, try a few of these more popular web sites:

- Spotlight English
- Ello
- Voice of America

Regardless of the listening technique you use in your English conversations, the point is to be involved in the present moment. It's difficult to advance your ability to speak English when you're thinking of your grocery list while the other person is speaking. Of course, this is excellent advice for everyone in a conversation whether he's learning the language or speaking his native tongue.

If you've been doing this and still frustrated in what you perceive as a lack of progress, then you'll be interested in learning the incredible breakthrough technique in the following chapter. It's called shadowing and in a moment you'll learn why.

Chapter 6: Shadowing

Pedro sat down for a cup of coffee with a friend. "I've hit a major snag in my ability to speak English," he said. "I've hit this brick wall and can't seem to breakthrough it. I'm not quite sure what to do."

The English student made sure he was talking to his friend in English. He also was attentive when his friend answered in English. "I know you're doing everything right," his friend replied. "You're being an active listener right now."

"So what's my problem?" Pedro asked.

"Perhaps you should try a technique called shadowing," his friend suggested. "Have you ever heard of it?"

Pedro shook his head no.

If, like Pedro, you don't know about the technique of shadowing, you may be missing that piece of the language puzzle that will pull your entire learning experience together and have you speaking English like a native in no time.

Shadowing is at least what this method is referred to in academic circles. Many others know it as "parroting." This learning method was originally developed in Germany and then later in Korea. It involves the awesome power of listening with the indispensable power of actually speaking the language.

It's an easy method to implement. You simply listen to a person who has a basic grasp of the language and you repeat – to the best of your ability – what he's saying. You do this immediately after the other individual (or recording) has spoken and you do this whether you understood all of his sentence or not.

According to Dr. Alexander Arguelles, the developer of this method, it's best to be repeating the words while you're walking. In doing so, he said you'll not only enhance your alertness but increase the oxygenation process of your body.

In fact, anyone; who has ever practiced this will testify that there is something – they aren't   quite sure what – about the walking (preferably outdoors) while you repeat what you hear. In fact, many individuals who have successfully performed this method describe it as the closest thing to listening to music and singing along.

No doubt you've done this. Every time you hear your favorite song, you can't help yourself, you end up singing along. If you pay close attention to what is occurring, you'll notice you're singing the words nearly at the same time as the musicians.

If you give this some thought it appears weird, especially because you probably couldn't recall the words unless you hear the start of the song. Then all the words come flooding into your memory without much effort. It's the same mechanism working when you shadow.

The peculiar aspect of learning a song is that you can go decades without hearing it or even thinking about it. The moment you hear even a portion of the tune, you're singing along with it like you heard it yesterday. All the lyrics come flooding back to your memory.

There are actually courses available to get you started. But as you decide whether you want to use them, you may want to try this on your own. This technique isn't that difficult with all the amazing technology that abounds. You can listen to almost anything on your cell phone, take a walk outside and parrot the words almost at the same time the recording is. You can do this with any material from recordings of speakers to audio books.

It's easy enough to get started. Decide on the English audio you'd like to use. If at all possible, choose selections that have an accompanying transcript or at the very least subtitles. The nature of the material doesn't matter. If you have a favorite movie, by all means choose that. You really couldn't get bored when you're watching and listening to something you enjoy.

Perhaps you have a favorite television show – either a crime drama or a situation comedy. Some individuals recommend such sites as Power English Lessons. You may want to give that site a try.

Prior to actually shadowing this material, you'll be wise to listen through it once without shadowing it to get acquainted with the content. This is especially true if you've never heard it before. It's actually a bit easier to shadow if you have at least a passing familiarity with the piece.

The Process of Shadowing

Once you've initially reviewed the material, start listening to it again. This time your goal is to imitate or parrot the actors and narrator as precisely as possible. The ultimate goal is to repeat everything they're saying.

Ideally, you'll want to say everything they're saying at precisely the same time as the recording. If at first you're not that familiar with the content, you can wait until the sentence is complete before repeating it.

When parroting the words don't just say them without any feeling. Imitate everything the native speaker is saying, down to the precise pronunciation, the inflection in the voices. If you try to be perfect in all of this, you'll drive yourself stir crazy.

Your goal is to try to keep up. The more often you shadow this material, the better you'll get. So instead of trying to perfect your presentation right from the start, just make up your mind you're going to have fun with this.

Below is an alternative to this specific approach to shadowing which may be more suited to your needs.

1. Start with finding a text at your spoken proficiency level in English.

2. Listen to this once in order to gain a general understanding of it.

This is a great step that many students try to skip only to find they need to stop and perform this ritual from the start – and this time listening to it before you shadow it. First, you'll know for certain if the chosen text really does match your proficiency level.

Secondly, you'll discover if the topic holds your interest. There's nothing worse than try to read something in a language that's not your native language and find it's . . . well, boring. If either of these is the case – too difficult or too boring – then go back and select another text.

3. Listen to the piece a couple of more times.

When you do this, you'll be sure to be confident in your ability to know what the text is talking about. You don't have to fully understand everything *before* you shadow it, but at least you know you'll eventually be able to figure it out.

4. If there are any words you don't know the meaning of look them up before going any farther.

That's right! Before you start shadowing look up the words you aren't positive you know. It may take a little more time, upfront before you shadow, but I promise you it'll save you time later in the exercise.

5. Listen to the text at least once a day.

Listen more than this if it's at all possible.

6. Pronounce the same piece until you can repeat it at the same speed as the recording.

7. Move on to another piece in the English language.

Approach the second piece in the same manner as you did the first.

Why Walking and Talking?

While you're shadowing remember that the ultimate way for this to work is by walking – preferably outside – while you're repeating the language. Don't overlook this seemingly inconspicuous aspect of this exercise. Why is this so important? According to some, and you probably have experienced this yourself, it's actually quite difficult to have your brain focus on learning a language while your body is trying to walk.

Think back to when you were learning how to drive. If you were like most of us, the first several times you were behind the wheel of a car you didn't talk much. You probably turned the radio or CD player down or even off as well. Once you conquered the act of driving, though, you felt much more comfortable listening to music or talking to your passengers.

There's a very good reason for this. It's difficult for the human mind to speak a language you're unfamiliar with and perform another activity. While at first you'll find this next to impossible (but don't give up on it) as you continue, you'll see improvement.

Shadowing while you're walking is challenging your brain. It's forcing your mind to understand new language skills and eventually train your body to accept speaking this language as an automated process. That in the end is exactly what you want: to speak English without giving it a second thought.

The Scriptorium Method

At about the same time Dr. Arguelles developed shadowing, he also created a related method for learning the spoken word. This technique, by contrast, combines the power of repeating words out loud with of the reinforcement of writing them on paper. It's called the *scriptorium method* and you may already be unwittingly using it. It might even be a method you've used in your native language as a youngster learning spelling words.

Instead of just working with words, you'll be working with sentences at least initially. Create a sentence or choose one you've already learned. Get a piece of lined notebook paper and begin writing the sentence. Instead of writing it all at once, however, write it deliberately. As you copy each word, pause momentarily and say the word out loud. Then – and only then – can you continue to the next word.

If, for example, you were using the first line of Charles Dickens' **A Tale of Two Cities,** you would use this sentence: "It was the best of times; it was the worst of times." Now grab your pen and paper and begin. Write the word it, pause and then say it. Do the same for "was." Write it down and pronounce it. Write and speak each word in the sentence until you've completed the each word.

No, you aren't quite done – not yet at least. Now that you've written it on the page say the entire sentence out loud. Pause for a moment. Do this again with the same sentence a minimum of ten to fifteen times. That purpose of this exercise isn't simply to recognize the words when you see them, but to actively speak them.

If you want you can now move on to another sentence. Some individuals choose to work from the sentences of a novel like this (although **A Tale of Two Cities** would take quite a while). Another option would be to copy and recite sentences from any of your lessons.

This is a great secondary method of learning pronunciation, especially if the option of shadowing is unavailable to you. The aim of writing and pronouncing words, like in shadowing, uses more than one sensory organ of your body. By combining these organs, you'll be increasing the chances that you'll remember not only the structure of the sentences, but the pronunciation of the words.

Use this interactive approach to the English language as often as you can fit it into your allotted time to study. You'll be amazed at how much faster you'll learn how to speak the language simply by writing and pronouncing your words and phrases once a week.

In the next chapter you'll learn one simple habit that just about all successful English students have used at one time in order to improve the ability to speak English and sound like a native.

Chapter 7: Secrets of a Fluent English Speaker

If you've been struggling with soaring to the next level of the spoken English language, then you may have already been asking yourself this one question, "What are those students who are excelling in this area doing that I'm not?"

And you're right to ask that question. That's the only way you can diagnose what you're doing compared to what they're doing. Here's a surprise. Usually it comes down to one exercise. One simple ten-minute exercise to be exact. This habit helps to thoroughly immerse these individuals in the language.

This chapter explains how you can use this incredibly powerful tool to aid you in soaring to the next level of fluency in speaking English.

Read a Book (Yes, in English!) out loud

What if you knew that there were one simple exercise that could totally transform the way you spoke the English language? That if you participated in this routine every day for as little as ten minutes, you'd be building your English speaking ability, not unlike an athlete improves his skill through daily practice?

Imagine what it would be like to speak the English language like a native without even the need to venture into any conversation with another person? If this sounds too good to be true, think again. You're about to be introduced to a simple ten-minute daily method that will do just that.

Not only that but this simple method can help you keep up in those conversations among native speakers who ordinarily speak so fast that most students get lost and even discouraged.

Simply reading a book written in English out loud. Yes, that's all there is to it. But there are a few criteria that go along with this exercise. The first caveat is that you have to read the words as fast as you can while retaining proper pronunciation. At first this may seem like you're reading at a snail's pace, but as you continue to practice you'll find yourself getting faster and comprehending the words more quickly.

Part of the key to this is the careful and deliberate pronunciation of words. Keep in mind that pronunciation depends on you to open and move your mouth properly. When you pay attention to the movement of your mouth, you'll be pleasantly surprised at the improvement in your pronunciation.

Many individuals try this suggestion but are, quite frankly, just a bit skeptical of it. They're not quite sure how reading a book out loud – to no one in particular, in fact could increase their skill. So why does it work?

1. This exercise is doing nothing less than creating an oral atmosphere around you.

If you're anything like the average student learning English as a second language, English is probably seldom if ever spoken in your home. This exercise, then, is an awesome way to practice speaking the language when you aren't in touch with others who speak it, even on a rudimentary level.

Try to invest at least ten minutes daily reading out loud five days a week. In fact, why not try it for a month. At the end of the month, see if you notice any changes in your fluency.

2. Reading out loud increases your opportunity for retention.

Not only does it increases your chances to retain more of what you read, you increase this opportunity by approximately 100 percent when compared to reading silently. When you read silently you use two parts of your body – your brain and your eyes. While this is good, reading out loud actually doubles the number of body parts involved in the process. This activity forces you to not only use your brain and your eyes but your ears and voice as well.

Scientists have discovered that this really does double your retention of the material. You're not only thinking about the language and seeing it, but you're also hearing it and saying it.

There is possibly no better way to actually immerse yourself in the English language. While you're reading you're actually subconsciously soaking up the thinking and speech patterns of the language. But that's not all, you're also enhancing your ability to remember in English as well as communicate in the language.

3. You're exercising your facial muscles.

Yes, this isn't the most exciting result of this habit, but it is more important than you think. The sounds involved in speaking the English language are formed through the passing of the air through a certain segment of our facial organs.

As you probably already know through your studies, the sounds are then formed through the use of your lips, nose, teeth, tongue and other facial features. When you're learning a new language, there are many new sounds you need to learn in order to speak it properly. At first it may seem that you're totally incapable of pronouncing certain sounds.

Many individuals whose first language is Spanish have a difficulty enunciating the letter "z" in English. Spanish doesn't contain that sound. But just for your information, native English speakers sometimes have a hard time with the "rr" sound of Spanish. This is not a natural sound for them to use. In each case, the individual needs to develop the specific muscles for proper pronunciation.

4. You'll learn how to become responsible for correcting yourself.

You've been studying the English language that you're already fairly proficient in the proper enunciation of it. Don't be surprised that as you read out loud, you'll slowly begin to "police yourself."

Eventually you'll hear yourself pronounce one or more of the words incorrectly. When you first start this habit, you may slide by this. After you're established in this habit, though, you'll discover yourself, stopping and pronouncing it again properly. That's exactly one of the goals of this exercise.

5. Reading out loud increases your oral fluency.

There's no way around it, reading a book or newspaper out loud must improve your fluency in English. Ideally, you'll want to take time out of your morning to read out loud. And yes, I do mention this for a reason. This short, simple exercise loosens your speech organs, getting them accustomed to making the sounds of English.

Not only that, doing it before class jogs your memory of the sounds necessary for the language. You'll soon discover that your fluency will be greatly enhanced on those days you take the time to do this exercise.

One of the great things about this exercise, you can choose a book that actually interests you. Choose a novel you've always wanted to read or one of your favorite authors. If you're a sports fan, for example, then you could read an autobiography of your favorite athlete or merely read the sports section of the newspaper daily.

Remember, though, that you'll gain the most from this exercise when you read actively or observantly. What do I mean by that? Be totally involved in what you're reading. Use your mind taking note of not only the material being presented, but the structure of the sentences as well the order of the words in sentences. Ideally, you'll transfer these observations into your daily practices. And the next thing you know you're speaking English like you were born into it.

Chapter 8: Idioms and More: You Can't be Fluent without Idioms

Hmm? Did you notice that title of this chapter? Yes part of it is what's known as an idiom. In fact, that's probably one of the most common idioms native speakers use.

The English language can be a struggle to learn on its own. Throw in an unexpected idiom or two and now you've opened a whole new can of worms. There again, is another idiom. Just for your information, opening a whole new can of worms means that in an attempt to solve one problem an entirely different problem popped up.

Even children who are native to the language have a difficult time learning some of the idioms if they've never heard them before. When I was a child, for example, and an older one at that, my mom and I were finishing up washing the dishes after supper one day. My father, who had gone into the living to read a book, actually fell asleep reading it. The book lay on his chest.

Mom said to me. I need to "take a page from Dad's book." I was horrified. "But, Mom," I said, "that would confuse him to no end." My mother looked at me like I was crazy. She was using an idiom and I was taking her words literally. I thought she was going to pull a prank on my father by actually confusing him by tearing a physical page from the book he was currently reading. As an avid reader, I didn't even say where the humor was in the act. What she meant, though, was that she was going to follow his example and take a nap.

Knowing the confusion I had with several idioms, who knew as I got older that I actually confused my own child with one. I said to her, in all innocence one time, that something I did would undoubtedly get her Dad's goat. She said to me (as if I weren't already aware of it), "But Mom, Dad doesn't have a goat."

Now as you probably have already guessed getting someone's goat has nothing to do with stealing his farm livestock. What I meant by that was I was going to agitate him, get him worried and perhaps even a little concerned about something. But my daughter, like myself before her, had to learn the language one idiom at a time.

How to Learn Idioms

Right now you're probably thinking that an idiom is a secret joke that native speakers like to pull on non-native speakers and children. Who knows? Perhaps that's exactly how idioms did come into use hundreds of years ago. Now there they are common phrases that are widely accepted in the English.

Unfortunately for the serious student of English, there is really no way to learn them except by memorizing them one by one. While there are really probably hundreds of them, I'm providing you with the meanings of the ten most commonly used idioms in the English language.

These are the ones you're most likely to encounter as you begin to delve deeper into the language. If you can begin by learning these ten, you'll probably reduce your confusion of listening to native speakers by quite a bit. You'll then be able to focus more on the other parts of the conversations you're listening to.

10 of the Most Common Idioms

1. A piece of cake

You'll hear this quite a bit. "That test was a piece of cake," someone might say walking out of a classroom. That means that it presented no challenge to them. It represented , in fact, quite the opposite -- something easy to accomplish. Another, related idiom, meaning much the same thing is "easy as pie." Why anyone would compare a pie to something being easy isn't really understood, but at least you now know the meaning of both of these.

2. It cost an arm and a leg

That would be a gory financial transaction if you were to take this phrase literally. This idiom means the item being referred to was expensive. It's used nearly constantly in this language. In fact, you've probably already heard it.

A second idiom with a very similar meaning is "it broke the bank." It doesn't mean that the bank – whatever or wherever that might be – literally broke into pieces or that it ran out of money. The phrase just means the cost of the item was quite expensive. In both of these cases, many times the implication is that the cost is more than what the item is worth.

3. Break a leg

Believe it or not, this idiom means "good luck." It's especially used backstage in theaters just prior to actors going on stage. It's considered bad luck to say the phrase "good luck" back stage, but apparently it's all right to wish someone to break a bone. It's widely used outside of this venue as well. So the next time someone tells you to "break a leg" they really aren't hoping you trip and fall.

4. Let the cat out of the bag

Here's another curious phrase. After all, who would place a perfectly good cat in the bag in the first place? And who would care if the cat got out? This phrase's true meaning, though, is to reveal something that was meant to be kept a secret. When someone tells you something and you inadvertently tell another, you're "letting the cat out of the bag."

5. Hit the books

Idioms can certainly conjure up some bizarre images in the minds of those who aren't native speakers. Upon first hearing this, perhaps you had an image of students surrounding themselves with the textbooks they like least and physically punching and hitting them. What a strange way of releasing your anger. This phrase is really synonymous with the act of studying. Yes, it's that simple. Not nearly as colorful, though.

6. Hit the nail on the head

When you hear this one you may believe you're speaking to a carpenter. But that's not necessarily so. In fact, chances are good the person who uttered this expression has never even used a hammer in his life. Once again, like with all good idioms, it hasn't a single thing to do with the physical item it's referring to.

Instead it has everything to do with performing a right move, action, or even the proper interpretation of a fact or statistic. At least with this idiom it's nearly understandable how it might have got its start. When you take a hammer and hit the nail on the head, the nail glides perfectly into the wood. With the idiom, you've done everything right.

7. To scratch someone else's back.

You may also hear this phrase as "You scratch my back and I'll scratch yours." This doesn't mean that you'll be literally standing behind someone asking them exactly where there back itches and then he'll do the same for you. Although implied in this literal interpretation is that both individuals are helping the other.

This often-used idiom means that if you help your friend with a problem or out of a tight situation, he'll return the favor when you need something done.

8. When pigs fly

Can you imagine anything more ridiculous than looking up in the sky and seeing a pig fly? They definitely weren't designed with flight in mind – regardless of how they may in evolve in the future.

So just the idea of pigs flying is utterly ridiculous. And there you have it. That's the entire point of this idiom. When pigs fly refers to an event that is highly unlikely, if ever, to occur.

9. Bite off more than you can chew

Do you recognize this idiom from the title of this chapter? While this has nothing to do with eating, with a little thought, you might be able to figure it out. Imagine you're starved and have been waiting in a restaurant for a meal that's more than a little late. By the time you get your sandwich you grab it and take a huge bite. Unfortunately, it's a bit more than your mouth can handle and you find it extremely difficult to deal with this situation in a polite and mannered fashion.

While this has absolutely nothing to do with food, it has everything to do with your trying to attempt a feat that is just a bit beyond your capabilities. If you've ever volunteered to perform a project for work only to discover you don't have the knowledge or skill to complete it, then you've bitten off more than you can chew. You've taken on a project that is just too large or beyond your capability to handle at the moment.

Homophones, Homonyms and Homographs

Just when you think the English language can't get any more difficult to understand, someone has to start talking about homophones, homonyms and homographs. It's bad enough that each of these words sound and look so similar, just wait until you discover what each word represents. Learning about these categories of words alone will convince you, if you need any more evidence, that the English language is not the easiest language to learn.

So what are they and why in the world should you even learn them? Let's tackle them one by one. A homophone, also called a homonym, is a word that has at least two distinct, usually unrelated meanings but are pronounced the same in each situation. Sometimes they have the same spelling, but not necessarily.

What do we mean by that? Look at the word rose. "The rose bloomed today." Used in this sentence you know that the word is referring to a flower. But in the sentence, "Diana rose from her nap" means something entirely different, even though they are the same word, spelled the same way.

When you read these words in sentences, you're likely to immediately know the meaning intended. When you and others use them as part of the spoken language you may have to listen closely to know what the word means in the context that it's used.

The use of all types of homophones in the English language is just another good argument for something we talked about earlier in the book: learning to recognize phrases instead of just words.

If you only learned words singly in your early years of language study, you may be puzzled by the use of the word rose in either of those sentences. Depending on what you learned, you may very well be picturing a flower when a person said "rose" instead of the verb, meaning to get up.

As you progress in your study, you'll recognize more and more of these. Here is just a small sampling of homophones:

Lacks – to be without something
Lax – not strict

See – to use your eyes
Sea – a body of water

Erie – one of the Great Lakes in the Midwest of the US
Eerie – a strange feeling, usually referring to something that is paranormal

Vein – blood vessels of mammals
Vain – to attempt something but have it not mean anything

Male – a man
Mail – letters that are delivered by the post office

On to Homographs

If you're not confused enough already, you just may be after you learn about words that are commonly called homographs. These words, more likely a pair of words, are normally spelled identically. The catch is they mean something different depending on their pronunciation. Again, these belong to a class that you'll discover as you continue speaking the English language tests not only your skills, but your patience as well.

Sometimes the pair of homographs are pronounced differently. The difference, however, is a subtle one. It's usually just a matter of the placement of the accent in the syllables that make up the word.

One thing you may want to know is that there exists an entire class of homographs that end in the three letters "ate." When they are pronounced one way they have one meaning and when you shift the accented syllable they mean something else.

A classic example of this is the word "advocate." When you pronounce it with the long "a" sound the meaning of the word is to be in support of something. When the word is pronounced with a short "a" sound, the word means a person who either supports or acts on behalf of the cause of another individual.

Unfortunately for the student of the English language these words are strewn all around. You'll never know where or when you might encounter them. But as you progress in your ability to speak the language you'll discover that you'll become much more familiar with them and recognize them when you both read and listen to the language. Below are just a few of the more common homographs you may encounter in your studies:

- **Attribute:** a characteristic or quality of something or to assign a characteristic to a specific person, place or thing
- **Axes:** the plural of the noun ax or the plural of the noun axis
- **Bass:** a deep tone or a type of fish
- **Bat:** a piece of equipment used to hit a baseball or the winged mammal
- **Compact:** something small or to make something small. It also refers to a case that holds make up. Additionally, you'll occasionally find this word meaning

agreement or covenant, as in the historic Mayflower Compact.

- **Compound:** something created from more than one substance or an enclosed area that includes at least one building
- **Content:** Satisfied or something that is found in an enclosed case. It also means the words found in books or other material
- **Desert:** an arid, dry place; to leave someone behind. Not to be confused with dessert, which is a sweet after-dinner treat.
- **Does:** a form of the verb do; the plural of doe, a female deer
- **Down:** the opposite of up or soft, young feathers of birds
- **Entrance:** the area in which you enter a room or to bewitch or delight an individual
- **Fine:** sharp or very thin or the penalty you pay
- **Lead:** to take a group behind you and show them the way or a type of metal
- **Minute:** 60 seconds or a portion of an hour
- **Object:** another word for anything you can see or touch or to speak up against something
- **Produce:** fresh fruits and vegetables as in the produce department of a grocery store or to create something
- **Refuse:** a verb meaning to decline something or a noun referring to garbage or waste
- **Row:** a fight or to move a boat with oars
- **Second:** a portion of a minute or the item after the first
- **Tear:** the water that comes from the eyes or to rip
- **Wind:** moving air or to turn in a circular motion
- **Wound:** an injury or something that has been turned, the past tense of wind

While much of this information is important in the written language, it's also fundamental to your acquiring better skills when it comes to the spoken word. If you hear one of these words spoken and need to take time out of your listening trying to decide what it means, you're also losing vital listening time for other portions of the conversation. In fact, in doing that, you may be missing the most important parts of the conversation.

Chapter 9: Contractions in the English Language

One thing you've undoubtedly discovered about the English language is its apparent randomness. As soon as you learn a grammatical rule or a way to pronounce a word you discover at least one exception to the rule. There you are thinking you were making progress. Now you're only left confused.

While it may not make you feel any better but everyone who learns this language has the same problems. We've already mentioned even native speakers have encountered these same problems and some of them have never fully conquered them.

One of the idiosyncrasies of the English language – and one that seems to confuse many students – is the contraction. Students and native speakers alike have problems knowing when to use them and when not to. Some individuals have problems knowing what the contraction even stands for.

If you're having these problems or try to avoid speaking with contractions for fear of making a fool of yourself join the club. But now, we're going to give you a quick course in this unique part of the English language. Before you've completed this chapter you'll be not only using contractions like a native speaker, but you'll know exactly why and how you're using them.

What is a contraction, anyway?

In its basic form a contraction is a shortened form of a word or two words. It's created, in its most common written form by omitted a letter or letters and replacing them with an apostrophe.

Contractions are normally used in spoken English. Not always found in the written language, a contraction represents syllables that have been dropped by native speakers because on the whole they speak fast and simply compress the words together. One of the ones you've probably encounter frequently is "can't" for "cannot."

You may already be using this one and a few others. They are after all, a more informal way to speak and they actually make you sound more like a native speaker. You're less likely to find them in the written language except in some informally written books, like this one whose writing style is to sound more conversational.

Essentially, English uses two types of contractions. The first variety is the type we've just defined, in which one or more letters are missing and replaced by an apostrophe. The list below contains a comprehensive list of contractions you may hear people speak, but it's not necessarily complete.

These contractions have been used for hundreds of years and agreed upon as it were by speakers of the English language. Due to the possibility of being misunderstood, it's widely accepted in the spoken language that individuals don't randomly create their own set of contractions. While these words are definitely the informal presentation of two words they are widely accepted by linguists.

Below are many contractions and the words they represent:

Contraction	Original
aren't	are not
can't	cannot
couldn't	could not
didn't	did not
doesn't	does not
don't	do not
hadn't	had not
hasn't	has not
haven't	have not
he'd	he had, he would
he'll	he will, he shall
he's	he is, he has
I'd	I had, I would
I'll	I will, I shall
I'm	I am
I've	I have
isn't	is not
it's	it is, it has
let's	let us
mustn't	must not
shan't	shall not
she'd	she had, she would
she'll	she will, she shall
she's	she is, she has
shouldn't	should not

that's	that is, that has
there's	there is, there has
they'd	they had, they would
they'll	they will, they shall
they're	they are
they've	they have
we'd	we had, we would
we're	we are
we've	we have
weren't	were not
what'll	what will, what shall
what're	what are
what's	what is, what has
what've	what have
where's	where is, where has
who'd	who had, who would
who'll	who will, who shall
who're	who are
who's	who is, who has
who've	who have
won't	will not
wouldn't	would not
you'd	you had, you would
you'll	you will, you shall
you're	you are
you've	you have

n

There's technically one other form of contraction, even though few people ever refer to it as such. That's the contractions that

English uses in front of full names to identify gender or occupation. In these, only a few letters of the original word is used and when writing them English rules state you place a period at the end. They should cause you absolutely no problem when you're speaking the language, just be aware of the pronunciation if you read any material aloud in your daily practice.

Mr.	Mister
Mrs.	Mistress
Dr.	Doctor
Atty.	Attorney
Rev.	Reverend

Learning contractions will go a long way in helping you to speak the English language more fluently. In fact, once you feel comfortable and confident using them – as well as understanding others who use them – you'll be well on your way to speaking the language like a native.

Conclusion

At this point of the book, you may be tempted to say that you've finished reading about breaking through to the new level of fluency in the English language. And you're certainly have completed the reading portion of this vital journey. However, you're far from completing your journey.

In one of the most vital ways, you've only just begun. Now that you know what it takes to learn how to reach that breakthrough level of the spoken English language, there will be no stopping you. You're beginning your journey of submerging yourself in English, taking up the challenge of speaking it whenever and wherever you can.

Congratulations. You've made a wise decision to continue to work toward your goals and not allowing anything to hold you back. Armed with the guidelines, suggestions, tips and techniques in this book and your own personal study and speaking habits that have been successful for you, you'll discover great success.

If your goal is to get a promotion at work, you can rest assured you'll be one of the prime candidates. If your goal is to earn better grades in school, you'll discover the aid in this book will provide you with the foundation you need.

Or perhaps you're learning English simply because your children are beginning to learn it in school. In any case, it's a skill that will be most vital to your future.

There are as many reasons for learning the English language as there are individuals using it. Regardless of your reason for learning it, you'll discover that once you put your mind to it, you'll have no problem.

If, any time along your journey, you feel as if you can't take another step or don't know how to go any further, simply open this book again and begin referring to it. Haven't been shadowing like you used to? Perhaps that's why you should be doing once again to breakthrough to yet another level of fluency.

Sometimes we get so involved in the day-to-day activities of life, that we forget to spend the time on goals that mean a lot to us. Sometimes we lose the ardor and excitement we had when we first started the project. If you believe that this is happening to you, why not just review one more time why you wanted to speak English in the first place. Review with yourself why you wanted to speak it as if it were your first language.

Of course, it's natural to feel a bit frustrated by the brick wall you seem to have it if you're feel as if you're not progressing in Of course, it's natural to feel a bit frustrated by the brick wall you seem to have it if you're feel as if you're not progressing in your pursuit.

This is the perfect time to refer to your S.M.A.R.T. goals again. When you read over these again, try to capture the excitement you felt when you originally wrote them. Hopefully, the goals were internally stimulated. That means you created them because you felt deeply serious about pursuing them for your own reasons.

If your reasons were because others were telling you that was what you should be doing, then it will be more difficult to recapture that magic that you initially felt. Even if they were externally stimulated, chances are that you felt so confident while learning the language that you adapted these goals as an internal challenge for yourself.

Here are two tips to help you stay with the program, as the English idiom goes:

You've already set your S.M.A.R.T. goals. Initially it really didn't matter the language. But now use both languages but don't stop there. From these goals, create what many would call a vision board. Remember earlier in the book, we used the goal of being able to give a presentation at work. Write this goal out and then find a photo of a boardroom or an office to represent the presentation and the desire to progress in your career.

If your desire was to keep up with your children's increasing knowledge of the English language which they learning at school, then take a photo of them and put next to that goal. You get the idea. Doing just this will revitalize you.

But then how do you maintain this excitement? Make sure you place these boards in a location in which you can see them, even briefly on a daily basis.

Each time you do see it, repeat your goal out loud. You may even want to stop for a moment and reflect on what this goal means not only to you but to your entire family.

Imagine how proud your children will be of you, for example, when you visit their teachers on the next parent-teacher conference day, speaking like a native speaker. Imagine how your career will soar when you improve your English enough to actually in front of your supervisors and colleagues and talk about the project in English.

Want to Go that Extra Step with Reminders?

Why not take advantage of the current state of technology and set daily or periodic reminders on your phone of what your true goals are in your studies. If you reflect at least once daily at a specific time every day, you'll be keeping these goals in your consciousness. In this way, you'll be less likely to get depressed over your studies and more likely to stay enthusiastic and centered.

Well Done! Look how far you've come since you took your first step. Remember to have a consistent English practice schedule everyday. Keep up the good work. Before you know it, you'll be speaking fluent English like a native.

Thank you for reading " English Fluency For Advanced English Speaker ". If you find this book helpful. Please take some time to share your thoughts and post a review on Amazon. It'd be greatly appreciated.

Remember: immersion is the key to learn any language. If you find yourself thinking in English, you are on the right track!

I wish you the best and good luck!

Whitney Nelson

Made in the USA
San Bernardino, CA
01 February 2017